NORDIC
DESIGNS COLORING BOOK

JESSICA MAZURKIEWICZ

DOVER PUBLICATIONS, INC.
MINEOLA, NEW YORK

Bibliographical Note

Nordic Designs Coloring Book is a new work, first published
by Dover Publications, Inc., in 2015.

International Standard Book Number

ISBN-13: 978-0-486-80354-8
ISBN-10: 0-486-80354-6

Manufactured in the United States by RR Donnelley
80354604   2015
www.doverpublications.com